SPIRIT MOTHER

Experience the Myth

A collection of nature poetry inspired by myth, folklore and legend

by

Patricia M Osborne

First published 2022 by The Hedgehog Poetry Press

Published in the UK by
The Hedgehog Poetry Press
5, Coppack House
Churchill Avenue
Clevedon
BS21 6QW

www.hedgehogpress.co.uk

ISBN: 978-1-913499-78-5

Copyright © Patricia M Osborne 2022

The right of Patricia M Osborne to be identified as the author of this work has been asserted in accordance with the Copyright, Designs and Patents Act 1988.

All rights reserved. No part of this publication may be reproduced, stored in or introduced into a retrieval system, or transmitted in any form, or by any means (electronic, mechanical, photocopying, recording or otherwise) without prior written permissions of the publisher. Any person who does any unauthorised act in relation to this publication may be liable for criminal prosecution and civil claims for damages.

9 8 7 6 5 4 3 2 1

A CIP Catalogue record for this book is available from the British Library.

Discover folklore about oak and mistletoe, and legends around lavender, white lily, amaryllis, banyan, rowan and hazel. Be surprised at how the nightingale got its sweet voice or how the devil tricked a fisherman. Be enchanted as you chase each mythical tale. Experience the myth as you turn the page.

Contents

White Lily 9
Amaryllis 10
Good Luck Charm 11
Blood of Dragons 12
Devil's Darning Needle 13
Aster 14
Cypress Tree 15
Galanthus 16
Lavender 17
Faceless Bird 18
Gift from the Gods 19
Atys the Phrygian Shepherd 20
Linden Oak 21
Lucerna 24
Nightingale Guardian 25
Nanabozho's Rainbow 26
Sacred Tree 28
The Cupbearer 30
Sequence - The Tree of Knowledge 32
Arthur 36
Sequence - Tree of Life 37

In Memory

of my dearest mum

Lila (1932-2014)

And Sister,

Heather (1956-2009)

Two courageous and inspiring women.

A light went out in my heart when you both left this world.

WHITE LILY

Hera puts her baby
to the breast,
beads of milk fall
to earth and spring
up as soft-white
trumpet blooms.

AMARYLLIS

To win the shepherd
you must pierce your heart
with a golden arrow
and make the journey
to his home each day until
you claim his love

Blood dripped as she journeyed the path
day on day to the shepherd's home,

shedding more and more from her open wound,
darkened stains seeding the fertile earth.

On the thirtieth day, blood-red blooms brushed
her ankles.

Astounded by their beauty,

Amaryllis
gathered an armful

of these new scarlet flowers.

Standing in his doorway, transfixed,
Alteo's dark brown eyes glistened.
Beguiled,
he inhaled
the precious gift,
pulled Amaryllis close

and tasted her lips.

She touched her chest,
pain free
since he'd kissed her wound,
the arrow's fissure
healed.

Alteo named
the posy–
blood from her heart.

GOOD LUCK CHARM

The yellowhammer perches
on the wine-red hedgerow,
holds his sunshine head high,
opens his black beak
and chortles my good fortune.

Showing off his chestnut rump,
                                                    he spreads his wings
to take flight,
        reveals his long white feathered tail
                                    as he glides across the sky
with a promise to cure my ills.

To see a yellowhammer brings luck and healing qualities.

BLOOD OF DRAGONS

Three golden apples swing from their bough,
guarded by Ladon, day and night weaving
his many heads around the twisted trunk.

As darkness falls footsteps creep from behind.

Hercules appears disguised as a lion,
feline teeth chattering on his neck chain.

The predator releases an arrow,
pierces Ladon's chest.

Left breathless and weak,
the dragon is grabbed
by the base of his hundred heads
in a stranglehold –

His pulse wanes.

Stabbed and throttled,
Ladon's veins seep rich-red blood
into the earth choking roots and plants.

Giant fists punch up through dirt.

A wide-girthed silver trunk rises
towards the sky, its spiky, emerald canopy
shields soil from the sun.

Reborn, Ladon thrives immortal in Dracaena
as crimson sap drips down his steel-grey bark.

DEVIL'S DARNING NEEDLE

After a   rebuke
        from the fisherman
the demon transforms
        his blood-red guise.

He wriggles   twists
       contorts his crooked body-

         gnarled limbs
            now six spindles

       horns - micro antennae
          re-emerges
             black and indigo

spreads   ice blue   iridescent wings

            angles backwards

         o   p   e
     r   l
  p   s

     over storm-rippled water

ASTER

Observe the night sky
watch the stars
listen for whispers
as the blue aster speaks
to her sisters.

CYPRESS TREE

Wandering through ghostly
ash and pine, Cyparissus tramples
broken branches calling out 'Peritas'
but there's no sign of the deer.

Bored because his pet
will not come out to play,
he dances in the grove,
draws back his bow,
releases the arrow.

The boy pounds the woods
to see what he has hit,
discovers his beloved Peritas
lying wounded, in pain.

He pleads to the god,
Apollo, 'Help me, my lover,
I've killed your precious gift.'

Cyparissus throws himself across
the pet's warm neck
as the stag exhales his last breath.

Apollo melds the bodies
of boy and deer–
transforming them.

Soft forest-green needles hang
from slender branches,
stretching to a narrow crown.

Pyramidal in shape,
the cypress tree is born.

GALANTHUS

I shelter at the base of trees,
abbeys, churchyards
or amongst woodland.

My neighbours, mistletoe,
petasites, wild aconitum,
hang close to my side.

I'm harvest for Norman Monks
who decorate churches
at Feast of Candlemas,

nature's medicine,
rub on temples
to treat *mal de tête*.

I spring into action,
push up through arctic-white
and cheer through winter gloom.

Standing with grace,
I nod as you pass
by silver birch.

Milk-tone drooping petals,
viridescent stem,

...symbol of purity.

LAVENDER

Two criminals seize a girl
as she scurries to the hills,
they tear her clothes, force
her to the ground,
gag her mouth
to silence her screams.

Left violated, distraught,
thrown in a heap on the earth,
her tears fall where she lies,
germinating blue and purple seeds.

FACELESS BIRD

A sprig lifts

        off the pavement

takes flight–

        a bird without a beak

            no face   no eyes

                no control of its fate.

Boreas's arms

        embrace the faceless bird

            until he's bored rigid

and drops the twig at my feet.

GIFT FROM THE GODS

Flickering shadows dance
around the campfire light.

Calian shuffles into the tepee
and hovers over a buffalo-robed bed.

His long dark braids shudder,
tears roll down his painted cheeks
as he strokes his young son's pale face.

He pleads to the gods
to spare Dyami, his firstborn.

Outside, chants stop,
replaced by gasps.

Calian clambers from the tent,
wipes his eyes,
looks up at the sugar maple
and spots a majestic bird
with a snow-feathered head
perched on the tree.

Orange talons cling to the branch,
yellow eyes stare down as he opens
his amber hooked beak.

He spreads his wings wide,
lifts his white fan-shaped tail
and soars high with Dyami's spirit.

ATYS THE PHRYGIAN SHEPHERD

Bitch. You'd think,
Rhea, Uranus's daughter,
would know better.

I shouldn't have cheated,
sure thing, fine, but to turn
me into a feekin' pine tree.

Under my prickly shade,
she's on her knees wailing,
wants me to forgive her,
for god's sake.

Zeus looks on,
catches her howls,
shafts me again,

promises my needles
will never shed,
keeping me evergreen.

Giving me no choice
but to be his mother's whore
whenever she chooses
to lie beneath me.

Zeus and Hermes, disguised as mortals, journeyed to earth for an adventure. After being rebuffed by locals they continued their journey.

LINDEN OAK

1.

White chitons brushed the beggars' ankles
as they ambled to the entrance
of a straw-roofed shack.

An elderly couple opened the door,
beckoned the strangers into their home.

Philemon poked the dying fire,
sparking a flame into ashen coals,

before he propped
up the lopsided table.

Baucis, his wife, waddled
to the stove
and boiled a pot of water.

Philemon poured wine –
the pitcher stayed full to the brim,
cup after cup.

Baucis gripped Philemon's arm,
her teeth chattered as she watched
the enchantment.

They huddled together whispering,
'But we have nothing, except...'
Philemon shrugged his shoulders,
went outside, returned
with their pet goose,
it wriggled from his hands.

Zeus and Hermes laughed
at the couple chasing the goose
until it took shelter
in the deities' arms.

2.

Zeus opened the cottage door
and bid the old folk look outside.
Eyes wide, the couple trembled,
gripping each other's hand

as a vast body of water swallowed
the land and locals' homes.

Philemon and Baucis sobbed
for their neighbours.

Zeus flung wide his arms.
'Do not weep
 for those mean mortals.

Fear not. We intend you no harm.
Wipe those tears and look.'

Sniffling, the couple dried their eyes.
A stone temple with a gold roof
stood before them.

Hermes patted Philemon's shoulder.
'A reward, for your kindness
and we grant you one wish.'

Bowing their heads,
the couple knelt before the gods
and answered,
'We wish never to be parted.'

3.

Leaves sprung from Philemon and Baucis
whilst recollecting shared love.

Bark enfolded the aged mortals
as they kissed goodbye.

Growing from the same trunk
linden and oak twisted, melding
the lovers for eternity.

LUCERNA

Feathered creatures nudge
and prod to be first in the queue
as God opens his paintbox.

He brushes the birds,
one by one,
in vibrant colours.

Transformed, they take flight,
boasting violet blues,
golden yellows
and burnished reds.

Hanging back, a small bird,
too shy to move forward,
stands alone in front of God

who shakes his head as he points
to the empty paint pots.

Lucerna lowers her beak
but God tilts the bird's chin –

Fear not, little one,
I gift you a perfect voice.

Orange haze descends the sky
as moonlight climbs.

God prompts the small creature to sing.

The nightingale opens her bill –
whistles a magical crescendo.

NIGHTINGALE GUARDIAN

Sunset reddens the sky
as daylight fades.

A brown feathered bird
inflates his buff breast
and begins a song.

His skirls warble
and he chirrups
a sweet tune

while standing guard
for the faery kingdom
living among hawthorn.

Night darkens,
white blossom dulls.

The nightingale salutes
a sprite with a whistle
all is well
for the city that hides
in the May tree.

Footsteps echo
through barren pasture,

the bird shoots
into the hedgerow
camouflaging his plume

and trills to a loud crescendo
alerting the enchanted realm–

NANABOZHO'S RAINBOW

Bluebird twins in the mood for mischief
        push out golden breasts,
lift azure plumage
        and
           swoop
            to the monochrome meadow

where they dip their wings and feet
into Nanabozho's cans of colour
        as he paints off-white blooms.

He transforms rambling roses crimson,
daffodil heads to burnished gold
and pansies to blossoms in every shade.

After being reprimanded by the painter
        the birds soar into the clouds
                to play another game.

                        Chasing
                each
            other
            they
            dive   in
                                          and   out
                    of a

                    waterfall

            red,
                orange,
                    yellow,
                        green,
                      blue,
                  indigo
                and
            violet

'Nanabozho's Rainbow' is based on a North American myth about Nanabozho, a culture hero, trickster and co-creator. This tale shows when Nanabozho was bored looking outside his window at the off-white flowers in the meadow and picked up his pots of paint to transform them.

SACRED TREE

In a subtle seduction,
Oak welcomes
Mistletoe's seed.

Evening reddens
the sky as drums beat
to a crescendo.

Entering the grove of oaks,
wreath-crowned druids parade
in gold, white, red,
clutching staffs.

One trails, bent,
a stringy silver beard falls
to his knees. He rings a bell.

Seers surround
the sun-god tree,
ivory candles ignite
one by one,
flames flit
in the breeze,
shadows flutter.

Drums mute.
Crickets chirp.
A snowy owl screeches
from a distant trunk.
Heads rise.

Deep breaths echo.

Priest, in white, ascends
the oak, unsheathes
the golden sickle strapped
to his back,
lops the stem
bearing milk berries.

Brothers clothed in gold catch
the twig in a cloak.

Drums pulsate,
beasts bellow,
eyes focus
on two white bulls
led by the horns.

A red-robed butcher
grips his blade, slits
one bull's throat
and then the other.
Crimson gore spurts
into the vessels,
metallic stench rises.

Drums cease.

Mistletoe glazed
with the bulls' blood
is blessed, offered
before the altar.

Sun-god's gift of semen
is embraced
by the earth goddess.

THE CUPBEARER

In Council the gods sip
nectar, devour ambrosia,
served by Hebe
from a carved chalice.

She leans
towards Olympus,
emerald taffeta rustles,
nut-brown ringlets brush
her slim neck.

Fixed by her beauty,
Olympus holds his stare.

Hebe's soft breasts swell
as she bends to pour the tincture
into his golden cup. Distracted
by Olympus' gaze, she trips
on her hem.

The magic chalice plummets,
punctures earth's core, settles
in a dim bleak realm
where souls dart
across grey fields of asphodel.

Morkaz, a faceless demon, catches Zeus' treasure,
hugs the trophy to his chest.

Zeus roars, releases his eagle, *Periphas,*
to retrieve the goblet of immortality.

Spreading her giant wings,
the messenger dives deep,
slips through a cleft
on the bank at *Lake Acheron*
into hidden gates of the underworld.

Along the *River Styx*, she glides
towards the demon and steals
the cup out of his hands.

Periphas thrusts upwards
through a portal, piercing
earth, towards heaven.

Morkaz leaps to the blue, lunges
towards the golden bird,
sinks his claws deep into flesh.

Raptor blood drizzles,
feathers float down
onto Mount Ada's plain

where rowan trees
spring up with polished barks
and jade arrowed leaves
adorning burnt amber berries.

SEQUENCE - THE TREE OF KNOWLEDGE

1.

Food of the Gods

Nine hazel trees throw shade
on a sunlit pool,
laden branches swing,
a cluster drops. Circles shimmer.

I nudge other salmon aside,
lunge to the top,
open my mouth to gulp hazelnuts.

On this daily diet
my golden coat glows
with red spots:
the world changes
before me.

My new gift of wisdom
makes me a prize.

News spreads
throughout lands.
Visitors are frequent,
asking advice
but I must be cautious.
Some desire my insight.

Too smart to be ambushed,
lily pads hide my bright fins.

One day sun soaks the pool,
I close my eyes and drift into sleep.

Awoken with splashes,
I swim towards my hiding hole
but-
       too late-

flapping my fins
I twist and squirm

trying to slip free.

2.

Young Fionn

'Fionn, a salmon gulps nuts
from hazel trees. His shining spots
mean far sight. What nonsense.

They say, first to taste will swallow
the knowledge. Some yarn.'
The druid master yawns,

taps his lips then waves
a map in my face. 'Supplies Fionn.'
The old man hastens us to go.

Traipsing far across
strange lands,
we trudge through sand,
marsh and meadow.
My bare feet sting.

Sunshine lights a small lagoon
almost hidden by a fringe of hazel trees.

The druid holds up his hand.
'Stop. This is the place.
Fionn –
go catch
the sacred salmon
for your master.'

Throwing off my shirt, I wade
into the sun-kissed pool,
cool water soothes my burnt feet.

I duck my head and search
silver depths.
A three-foot fish
luminates
ripples.
His black eyes stare,
threaten,
but I'm too fast,

I grab the monster.
It tries to slip through my hands.

'Master, quick.'

The old man dives in,
seizes the tail and belly
while I secure the jaw.

We scramble up the bank –

the spotted fish thrashes
until his strength wanes.

Picking up a large stone, I hammer
the revered salmon's head,
slice him with my knife.

3.

Master Druid

Foolish boy prepares
the fire and fish.
I rub
my hands
and smile.
The lad is naive,
no sense.

Fionn tosses
the salmon
onto the flame,
watches it spit.

He presses
the fish on its side,
burns his thumb,
raises it to suck.

'Don't,' I shout...

The wisdom of Belenos
floods his eyes.

End of Sequence

ARTHUR

A knight cheated death
when transformed with black magic
to a dark raven.

SEQUENCE - TREE OF LIFE

1.

Star-Shaped Birthmarks

Infants in corn-yellow slings
either side of her chest,
drag Hiranya down.

Tears fall from creased cheeks,
darkening her magenta headscarf.

She reaches a banyan,
stops under its towering canopy,
kisses the orphaned twins. 'I'm sorry.'

The old woman peers
up inside the twisted bark.

'Spirit Mother,
I come for help.

At dawn the rebel king
beheaded our righteous royals

and condemned
Prince Asav and Aryan
to death by drowning.

Please take these boys
into your care.

Draping white muslin
around their tender bodies,
Hiranya covers
the star-shaped birthmarks
on their curling arms, and lays
the babies under the banyan's shade.
The infants' dark eyes follow
the old woman as she shuffles away.

2.

Spirit Mother

Spirit Mother swishes her twisted side-shoots
caressing Asav and Aryan's tiny, waving arms.
Sap drips into their opened mouths.

Nurtured on Mother's milky leaves,
the babies push their limbs
against her bark.

Asav and Aryan roll,
draw up their knees to crawl,

become young boys who run.

Tangled trunks, roots and branches
shield them from blistering heat
and the tree blossoms with inflorescence.

3.

The Crowning

Ten-year-olds, Asav and Aryan,
charge around the shadowed arbour,
their high-flute squawks
mimicking jungle crows.

Marching towards the banyan
the Caddo tribe beat drums,
drop bright blankets
under the tree's shelter
to carpet their new home.

Head-dressed Khari brothers,
bring the boys to the chief.
Asav and Aryan wriggle
but the invaders
hold firm, pointing
to the star-shaped marks,
panting, 'The lost kingdom.'

Maidens with black braids
sway hips to the drumbeat
as they toss orange garlands
around the young boys' necks.

Face-painted youths
lift the noble pair,
chanting 'Aye yah yah,'
around a crackling fire.

Asav and Aryan
face each other,
clasp hands,
eyes wide,
lips tightly closed.

Tom-toms thump,
sitars strum,
mantras fill the Banyan.

Hiranya, an aged woman,
hobbles to the front,
she screams with pleasure,
hugs and kisses the orphans,
sits down behind them
to plait their straggly hair.

Four members of the tribe hoist
the twins onto bamboo thrones,
a chief places olive-foliage coronets
onto Asav and Ayran's small heads.

The young princes giggle.

Spirit Mother rustles her branches.

End of Sequence

ACKNOWLEDGEMENTS

Many thanks to the editors of the following publications in which these poems have previously been published:

Sacred Tree   *Ink Drinkers Poetry Quarterly* (2021)

Atys The Phyrgian Shepherd   *Flights* - Flight of the Dragonfly (2022)

Special thanks to Maureen Cullen, Sheena Bradley, Corinne Lawrence, Francesca Hunt and Suzi Bamblett, for their continued support and valuable feedback. Gratitude goes to Craig-Jordan-Baker at University of Brighton for pushing me to the next level in narrative poetry. Finally, I'd like to thank Mark Davidson at The Hedgehog Poetry Press for offering me this publishing opportunity and for being such an awesome editor to work with.

"*Spirit Mother* is a sensory voyage of discovery and delight through a rich landscape of Greek, Celtic, and Native American mythologies. The poems are by turns delicate and earthy, juxtaposing the sensual and sublime with the sharp and shocking to remarkable effect. The ancient feels at once eternal ('Galanthus') and starkly contemporary ('Lavender'), and the senses are fully engaged by a heady palette of shades, scents, sounds, and sensations. Patricia M Osborne has created a collection to be treasured - each poem imprints itself on the reader, and many will never leave."

Mary Ford Neal
Writer and Academic

"Spirit Mother offers the reader a compelling journey through a subtle plurality of viewpoints; a cumulative, unified and immensely powerful, life-affirming lens. Osborne employs all the writing skills which have earned her regular five-star accolades for her work over many years. You render yourself a clear disservice if missing out on this outstanding volume of poetry. Don't let that happen."

Brian McManus,
Reviewer, Writer, Pushcart nominated poet.

ABOUT PATRICIA M OSBORNE

Patricia M Osborne is married with grown-up children and grandchildren. Although Liverpudlian born she now lives in West Sussex. In 2019 she graduated with an MA in Creative Writing (University of Brighton).

Patricia is a published novelist, poet and short fiction writer. She has been published in various literary magazines and anthologies.

Patricia has a successful blog at Whitewingsbooks.com featuring other writers. When she isn't working on her own writing, she enjoys sharing her knowledge, acting as a mentor to fellow writers.

Previous poetry pamphlets published by The Hedgehog Poetry Press *Taxus Baccata,* (2020) *The Montefiore Bride* (2021) co-authored pamphlets - *Sherry & Sparkly* (2021*) Symbiosis* (2021)

www.ingramcontent.com/pod-product-compliance
Lightning Source LLC
Chambersburg PA
CBHW020035120526
44588CB00031B/832